TIGERS

Amy-Jane Beer

Grolier
an imprint of

www.scholastic.com/librarypublishing

Published 2009 by Grolier
An imprint of Scholastic Library Publishing
Old Sherman Turnpike, Danbury,
Connecticut 06816

For The Brown Reference Group plc
Project Editor: Jolyon Goddard
Picture Researcher: Clare Newman
Designers: Dave Allen, Jeni Child, John
Dinsdale, Lynne Ross, Sarah Williams
Managing Editors: Bridget Giles, Tim Harris

Volume ISBN-13: 978-0-7172-8035-3
Volume ISBN-10: 0-7172-8035-7

**Library of Congress
Cataloging-in-Publication Data**

Nature's children. Set 4.
    p. cm.
  Includes bibliographical references and
index.
  ISBN 13: 978-0-7172-8083-4
  ISBN 10: 0-7172-8083-7 ((set 4) : alk. paper)
  1. Animals--Encyclopedias, Juvenile. I.
Grolier (Firm)
  QL49.N385 2009
  590.3--dc22

                    2007046315

Printed and bound in China

PICTURE CREDITS

Front Cover: **Shutterstock**: Chris Sargent.

Back Cover: **Shutterstock**: Iconex; **Still
Pictures**: H. Schmidbauer.

Corbis: str/epa 41; **FLPA**: Martin Harvey
34, Gerard Lacz 33; **Nature PL**: Laurent
Geslin 46, E.A. Kuttapan 29, Anup Shah
2–3, 10, 30, 38; **NHPA**: Iain Green 22;
Photolibrary.com: Tom Brakefield 26–27,
Daniel Cox 42; **Shutterstock**: Karel Gallas
17, Eric Gevaert 9, Cindy Haggerty 13, Keith
Allen Hughes 21, Maxim Kazitov 5, Tan Kian
Khoon 14, Timothy Craig Lubcke 18, R. Gino
Santa Maria 45, Chris Sargent 37, Taolmor 4;
Still Pictures: H. Schmidbauer 6.

Contents

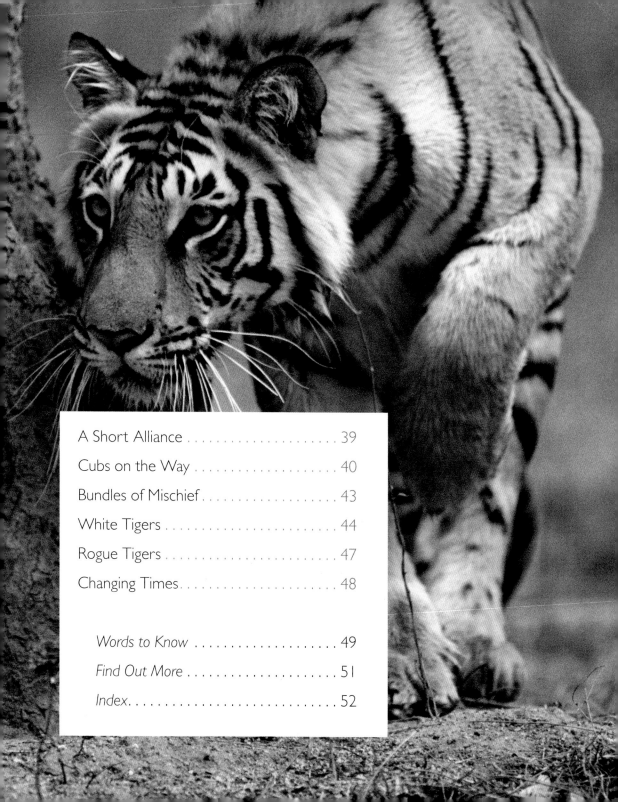

FACT FILE: Tigers

Class	Mammals (Mammalia)
Order	Carnivores (Carnivora)
Family	Cats (Felidae)
Genus	Tigers, lions, leopards, and jaguars (*Panthera*)
Species	Tiger (*Panthera tigris*)
World distribution	India, China, Southeast Asia, and Siberia
Habitat	Varied, from hot and humid tropical forests and swamps to the snowy wilderness of Siberia
Distinctive physical characteristics	Huge size; orange coat with vertical black stripes and white facial markings
Habits	Live alone except for mothers with cubs; active day and night; hunt live prey by stalking or ambush
Diet	Mainly large hoofed animals such as deer, antelope, and buffalo; also monkeys, birds, and sometimes humans

Introduction

The tiger's beautiful orange coat with black stripes has made it one of the most recognizable animals in the world. Its striking coat isn't just for show, however. The unique markings **camouflage** the cat in its forest home—allowing this fierce **predator** to creep up on **prey** unseen.

There is just one species of tiger. Scientists, however, have divided the tigers up into several kinds based upon where they live. Today, tigers are found in India, China, Southeast Asia, and Siberia. Each kind of tiger is slightly different from the others. The Siberian tiger, for example, is the biggest—in fact it is the biggest of all cats.

Historically, tigers were much more widespread, occurring in much of Asia.

With tail aloft, a Bengal tiger leaps. A tiger's tail, which may be up to 3 feet (90 cm) long helps the cat balance.

6

Crouching Tiger

In some ways, tigers are much like domestic cats. Have you ever watched a cat hunting? It moves in a stealthy, slow-motion stalk. Before pouncing it will tense, crouch, then suddenly attack its unsuspecting prey. Tigers hunt much the same way. They creep silently up on their victim before springing a surprise attack. A domestic cat will kill a mouse or rat with a bite to its neck. A tiger does the same, but its victims are usually much bigger, such as deer, bears, water buffalo, and cattle.

A surprise attack is not the tiger's only way of hunting. Often, a tiger will sit and wait patiently for prey to wander close by, before leaping out. This kind of hunting is called ambushing.

Home Range

Tigers have relatively simple needs—food, water, and shelter. A lot of different **habitats** in Asia provide these basic needs, and in the past these adaptable cats could be found across a huge **range**. They lived in dense jungles, swamps, plantations, open woodlands, and hilly and mountainous areas in regions such as Indonesia, India, China, and the vast wilderness of Siberia. Now, as their habitat has shrunk and their numbers have been reduced, they are found in only a few pockets within these regions.

In the hot southern parts of Asia, tigers tend to be smaller, with a thin, silky coat. In the north, tigers grow very large and their extremely thick coat of fur makes them look even bigger still.

The bold pattern on a tiger
breaks up its outline, thereby
helping to camouflage the
animal in its forest home.

There are more than 10,000 tigers in captivity. That's more than the number living in the wild.

Tigers Everywhere

Even though wild tigers are becoming rare, these striped cats can still be seen all over the world. They appear on television wildlife shows, at the movies, in books, on advertising boards, and even on cereal boxes. Tiger stripes also appear on clothes and in all sorts of designs. It seems humans can't get enough of these eye-catching big cats.

Perhaps the most famous piece of writing about this magnificent cat is William Blake's poem, "The Tiger." Another English writer deeply in awe of the tiger was Rudyard Kipling. He lived for many years in India and wrote *The Jungle Book.* In Kipling's story, a tiger named Shere Khan is portrayed as a cunning and powerful character.

One Mighty Cat

The tiger is known as a big cat, not just because of its size, but also because it has features in common with other big cats, such as lions, jaguars, leopards, and cheetahs. Most big cats are able to roar. They also have a circular pupil in each eye that shrinks to a small dot in bright light. Small cats, such as lynx, ocelots, and house cats, cannot roar, and their pupils close up to slits in bright light.

But tigers are not just big cats, they are the biggest species of cat alive today. The biggest tigers come from Siberia, where their massive bulk helps them keep warm. They can weigh up to 790 pounds (360 kg). That's as much as four or five men! Other tigers are smaller, but even the small ones are powerful enough to take down large deer with a swipe of their paw.

In winter, a Siberian tiger's coat changes color to match the snowy background.

13

Tigers can swim 3 to 4 miles (5 to 7 km) across huge rivers with no trouble.

Supreme Athlete

If there were Olympic Games for animals, the tiger would have a hard time choosing which event to enter. Sprint, long jump, wrestling, weight lifting, gymnastics, and swimming— a tiger would be a gold-medal contender for all of these events.

Tigers have long legs, especially at the back, which make them great runners. The huge muscles of the hindquarters allow the tiger to launch itself from a standing start into a 35 mile (55 km) per hour dash or into a leap of more than 30 feet (10 m) long! The front legs are slightly shorter, but still amazingly powerful. With its claws hooked into a victim's body, a tiger can bring down and kill animals weighing up to one ton (1 tonne) and then drag them away. Like other cats, tigers are extremely graceful, but unlike most cats they love water. They often enter water to cool off.

Colorful Cat

There's no mistaking a tiger's coat. No other animal has the same striped black and orange fur. The stripes are vertical on the body and horizontal on the legs and tail. The black markings frame the animal's face in a pattern that is as unique to a tiger as a fingerprint is to a human. In fact, the stripes on one side of a tiger's body are different from those on the other side.

Most tigers are orange with black stripes, have a pale belly, and white markings on the face. However, some are white with dark brown stripes. All tigers have black ear backs. Those help exaggerate movements of the ears. Tigers seem to use their ears for communicating. Just as a person might raise his or her eyebrows to show surprise or lower them in an angry glare, a tiger might flick its ears to show its mood.

To keep their fur in tip-top condition, tigers spend a lot of time cleaning, or grooming, themselves.

Sumatran tigers, such as this one, have the most whiskers of any type of tiger.

The Cat's Whiskers

Tigers have very long, stiff whiskers. Each one can be as thick as the lead in a pencil. Whiskers are special hairs. Like normal hairs, they sprout from cells called **follicles**. Whisker follicles are larger than regular follicles, and they are surrounded by nerve cells. When a whisker touches something, it bends. The nerves around the follicle feel the pressure and pass a signal to the tiger's brain. Using its whiskers, a tiger can feel its way around in the forest even in pitch darkness. Because the whiskers reach out about as wide as the tiger's body, the cat can tell if a gap is large enough for it to squeeze through—it is very rare for a tiger to get stuck!

Tiger Feet

With their claws retracted inside the toes, tigers
have surprisingly soft feet. Each foot has four
toes with springy pads, very similar to those on
a dog or cat, only much bigger, of course! The
pads allow the tiger to walk very quietly. The
skin covering the pads is rough, for good grip
and tough enough to protect the tiger from most
thorns and prickles on the forest floor.

In winter, Siberian tigers grow extra-thick
fur on their feet. Besides keeping the tiger's feet
warm, the furry paws act like snowshoes. They
spread out the weight of the big cat so it does
not sink too far into the deep snow.

A swipe from a Bengal tiger's large forepaw can kill most small prey.

21

A tiger's hooked claws are about 4 inches (10 cm) long. Tigers are excellent tree climbers thanks to their sharp claws and gripping paws.

Slashing Claws

Tigers are not only extremely powerful animals, they are also very well armed. Sheathed inside each toe—four on each foot—is a huge, hooked claw with a pin-sharp tip. The claws are the largest of any cat. They are about as long as a human finger. Each claw is made of keratin—the same substance as human fingernails, but much thicker and stronger. Even so, tigers have to look after their claws and protect them from wear and tear. A tiger does that by keeping its claws safely retracted most of the time. When fighting or trying to bring down prey, the claws spring out, allowing the tiger to slash and pierce the toughest animal skin.

Tiger Teeth

Tigers have awesome teeth. The largest are fanglike teeth called canines. There are two canines in each jaw. They are used to pierce the skin of prey when the tiger makes a kill. The Bengal tiger from India has the longest canines —up to 4 inches (10 cm)—of all tigers and other big cats. The small, sharp teeth at the front of the tiger's mouth are called incisors. They are used for grabbing and fine cutting. The rest of the teeth in a tiger's mouth are called premolars and molars. They have very sharp outer edges, and they are used for chopping up meat.

Tigers never eat vegetables or greens, so they don't need teeth for grinding. Their meaty meals are swallowed in big chunks—it's amazing they don't get indigestion!

Sandpaper Slurp

Have you ever been licked by a house cat? If so, you'll know its tongue is very rough—like warm, wet sandpaper. A tiger's tongue is the same, only bigger. The tongue contains a lot of muscles. The muscles are so powerful that once the tiger has torn into a carcass with its teeth and claws, it can strip out the meat using just its tongue. When a tiger has finished a meal, all that is left are clean bones and skin.

The tongue is also used for cleaning, or grooming. A tiger spends plenty of time looking after its fur, licking out the grime and grease. The tiger also grooms itself to remove parasites, such as ticks and leeches, that try to attach to its skin to feed on blood.

Tigers are one of the few cat species that don't mind getting wet. Tigers will even hunt prey such as crocodiles, water buffalo, and big fish in water.

In for the Kill

Tigers kill in three ways. Small prey, such as hares and birds, are struck down with a blow from one of the cat's mighty front paws and killed instantly. Usually, only young tigers bother with such small prey. Larger prey is knocked down and finished off with a bite to the back of the neck. A tiger's long canines bite through a vulnerable spot at the top of the prey's spine. The prey is killed very quickly.

Finally, for very large prey, such as antelope and buffalo, the tiger might have to use its full body weight to bring the prey to the ground. The tiger holds its prey down, while it gets a suffocating grip on the victim's throat. The tiger must be 100 percent sure the prey is dead before it lets go. Large animals like buffalo are not defenseless. If they manage to struggle to their feet when the tiger is on the ground, they can do serious damage, or even kill, with their horns and hooves.

A wild boar makes
a medium-sized meal
for a Bengal tiger.

29

A female tiger suffocates a chital deer. She holds on for several minutes until she is sure the deer is dead.

Private Dining

After a tiger makes a kill, it usually tries to take the prey somewhere private to eat. The smell of blood immediately begins to attract scavenging animals, such as vultures, wolves, and even other tigers. Therefore, a tiger with a big kill is always nervous. A tiger can eat up to 90 pounds (40 kg) of meat in one sitting, so an animal such as a small deer might only make one meal. But a large prey animal, such as an Asian buffalo, will feed the tiger for several days—if it can keep other meat eaters away. A tiger can drag prey much heavier than itself a mile or more to a suitable dining spot, usually a patch of dense vegetation.

What a Mix-up!

Lions and tigers rarely meet up in the wild. There are a few lions still living in India, but most lions live in Africa, where there are no tigers. However, in zoos and wildlife parks the two types of big cats can get together, and sometimes they **mate**.

The results are what zoologists—scientists who study animals—call **hybrids**. A hybrid is an offspring that is half one species and half a different species. These mixed-up big cats are called "**ligers**" and "**tigons**." (Ligers have a lion father and a tiger mother, while tigons have a tiger father and a lion mother.) Ligers and tigons usually look like what they are—a hotchpotch of lion and tiger. They have tawny fur with light stripes. The males have a short mane. Ligers can grow even bigger than their parents—when they rear up on their back legs, some are twice as tall as a man.

A tigon, such as this one, grows to about the same size as a lion or tiger. Ligers are usually bigger than either parent.

33

Two Bengal tigresses greet each other. Tigresses that have neighboring ranges are likely to be sisters, cousins, or mother and daughter.

Tiger Territory

Tigers live alone and prefer not to meet one another, but their **territories** often overlap. They leave scent marks around their territory so that other tigers know they are in the area. If two female tigers, or tigresses, meet, they might share a short greeting by rubbing cheeks. But they tend not to stay together long.

Male tigers are less tolerant of other males. The scent marks they leave say, "Stay out if you are an adult male, I live here!" Usually, these messages are respected and trespassers move on quickly. That is a surprisingly peaceful system for such fierce animals, but it makes good sense. Tigers seem well aware of their own deadly strength and they wisely avoid getting into fights whenever possible.

Dangerous Visitor

A tigress who is **nursing** young, or **cubs**, cannot become pregnant. That is nature's way of ensuring she doesn't end up with more young than she can care for. She will only be ready to breed again, when her cubs are grown up and ready to leave or if the cubs die. Male tigers instinctively know that, and given half a chance a male will try to kill any young cubs it comes across. Doing so speeds up the female's natural breeding cycle.

Of all the dangers faced by young cubs, adult male tigers are the most threatening. Mother tigers know that, and it makes them extremely aggressive toward strange male visitors. The scent of a male will put her on full alert, and if necessary, she will attack with such ferocity that most males back off immediately.

A Siberian tiger
snarls, baring its
impressive canines.

A Bengal tigress leaves scent from her face on a tree to mark out her territory.

A Short Alliance

When a female is ready and willing to breed, she lets the male tigers know by leaving special scent marks all over her territory. The scent contains chemicals called **pheromones** (FEHR-UH-MOANS), which male tigers can smell from a long way off.

   Usually, the male living closest to the female's territory will be first on the scene. Often, however, he'll have competition from other males, attracted to the area by the female's scent. Sometimes, the males will fight. In the end, it is the female that has the final say as to which male will be the father of her cubs. The unwanted males are then driven away. The winning male sticks around for a few days and mates several times with the female, but he soon leaves, too.

Cubs on the Way

Tigers are born in **litters** of between one and six, though two or three is most common. It takes a little more than three months for a litter of baby tigers to develop inside their mother. She gives birth to her cubs in a quiet place, such as a dense thicket, usually near the middle of her territory. For the first few weeks, the new family cannot travel far. Often, that means the female will lose parts of her territory to other tigers that notice that she has not been around.

The mother tiger feeds her young on milk for three months, then begins to offer them scraps of meat to taste. After about six months, the cubs eat only meat and show a keen interest in hunting, often getting in the way when trying to "help" their mother!

Newborn tiger
cubs weigh up to
4 pounds (1.8 kg).

Captive Siberian cubs nuzzle each other.
In the wild, only about 50 percent of cubs
survive to adulthood.

Bundles of Mischief

Tiger cubs spend most of their waking hours playing with their brothers and sisters. Sometimes, they get their mother to join in, too! They play chasing games and fighting games, with plenty of rough-and-tumble. The cubs also play hunting games, pretending to stalk leaves or other objects, before leaping with gusto to pin them to the ground. It all looks like great fun, but there is a serious side to all this playtime, too. Most games are imitations of real life. There will come a time when all the chasing, leaping, and pouncing will be essential for catching prey. The young cubs will most likely have to fight one day, too—either to protect their cubs or to win a mate.

White Tigers

Many zoos around the world keep white tigers. White tigers have white fur with black or brown stripes and blue eyes. They are not **albinos**, but they cannot produce the orange pigment, or coloring, that gives ordinary tigers their distinctive fur and fiery golden eyes. People often assume that white tigers come from Siberia, where their white coat would help them hide in snowy landscapes. But in fact, white tigers can turn up any place. They are extremely rare naturally—the last time anyone saw one in the wild was in 1958. Zoos, however, have made a special effort to breed them. All the white tigers in zoos around the world are the descendants of a single male Bengal tiger that was captured in 1951.

White tigers in zoos are very inbred and are, therefore, at risk of health problems.

Tigers will only turn
into man-eaters if
their natural prey
becomes scarce.

Rogue Tigers

In some parts of Asia, especially in India, tigers live close to large populations of humans. In the past, people would have killed tigers that came anywhere near villages. But now the tiger is a protected species, and they cannot be killed without a very good reason. Unfortunately, that means that some people are more in danger of being attacked by tigers now than ever before. Tiger attacks are most common in the Sunderbans swamps near Calcutta, India. The swamps cover a huge area and offer rich fishing. But the forested islands of the region are home to several hundred Bengal tigers, some of which have learned to think of humans as prey. The Sunderbans tigers kill about 100 people every year.

Changing Times

Wild tigers have disappeared from most areas of their former range. In many places they have died out because humans have felled the forests where they lived, for timber and to make way for farms and towns. Those tigers then starved because their prey, which also lived in the forests, disappeared, too.

In the past, tigers were also hunted. Local people trapped and killed them out of fear, while Indian princes and foreign hunters came to shoot them for sport. Now that tigers are rare, some people make a lot of money hunting them illegally and selling their skins and heads as trophies. Other body parts of tigers are used in Chinese medicine. But, fortunately, most people would now much rather shoot a tiger with their camera than with a gun. These days, tourists travel from all over the world to watch these awesome animals in the wild.

Words to Know

Albinos Animals with no pigment in their skin. Albinos have white hair and pink eyes.

Camouflage When an animal is difficult to see against a particular background because of its patterns and colors.

Cubs Baby tigers.

Follicles The bases where individual hairs are rooted in the skin.

Habitats The places where animals live.

Hybrids Animals or plants that are crosses between two different species.

Ligers Hybrids between a male lion and female tiger.

Litters Groups of baby animals born together to the same mother.

Mate	To come together to produce young; either of a breeding pair of animals.
Nursing	Feeding young mammals on milk from the mother's teats.
Pheromones	Chemicals given off by animals that tell others of the same type when they are ready to breed, for example.
Predator	An animal that hunts and eats other animals.
Prey	An animal hunted by other animals.
Range	The area in which a species or an individual animal lives.
Territories	Areas that animals defend as their own private space.
Tigons	Hybrids between a male tiger and female lion.

Find Out More

Books

Hirschi, R. *Lions, Tigers, and Bears: Why Are Big Predators So Rare?* Honesdale, Pennsylvania: Boyds Mills Press, 2007.

Squire, A. O. *Tigers.* True Books. Danbury, Connecticut: Children's Press, 2005.

Web sites

All About Tigers
www.enchantedlearning.com/subjects/mammals/tiger/
Tons of facts about tigers with links to printouts.

Creature Feature: Tigers
www.nationalgeographic.com/kids/creature_feature/0012/tigers.html
Fun facts, a video, an audio clip, and more.

Index